Define Your WIN

Wael Badawy PhD

ISBN-13: 978-0-9938703-2-3
ISBN-13: 978-0-9938703-3-0 Electronic Book

DEDICATION

To my wife Roya

and my children Saif, Seleem, Adam and Zain

without whom this book would have

been completed two years earlier.

To my Mother, Sister and late Father who believed in me
and inspired me to be who I am..

CONTENTS

ACKNOWLEDGMENTS

First and foremost, I would dedicate this book to my wife Roya.

I also thank my wonderful wife for the allowing me to spend much time in front of my computer.

I'd like to thank my parents for future gatherings as I'm sure they will all read it soon.

My business partners, especially to continue on in the Journey.

I thank each of them for the community they've created!

Thanks for everything. Thanks to the general community for using my concepts and providing great ideas and support via mailing lists; without this help I could not create newsletters and podcasts.

You were born to win, but to be a winner, you must plan to win, prepare to win, and expect to win.

Zig Ziglar

1. The Definition of WIN

WIN is a three characters word that consists of the letters "W", "I", and "N". In this chapter, we would will define WIN. Before defining "WIN", it is always recommended explore the definitions

$$W+I+N=WIN$$

of WIN. WIN is a noun, verb, and adjective.

Win is defined as

- ***Win(adj)*** to gain by superiority in competition or contest; to obtain by victory over competitors or rivals; as, to win the prize in a gate; to win money; to win a battle, or to win a country

- **_Win(adj)_** to allure to kindness; to bring to compliance; to gain or obtain, as by solicitation or courtship

- **_Win(adj)_** to gain over to one's side or party; to obtain the favor, friendship, or support of; to render friendly or approving; as, to win an enemy; to win a jury

- **_Win(adj)_** to come to by toil or effort; to reach; to overtake

- **_Win(adj)_** to extract, as ore or coal

- **_Win(verb)_** to gain the victory; to be successful; to triumph; to prevail

- **_Win(noun)_** _is_ An individual victory. _For example_: Our first win of the season put us in high spirits.

- **_Win(verb)_** To conquer, defeat.

- **_Win(verb)_** To triumph or achieve victory in (a game, a war, etc).

- **_Win(verb)_** To obtain (someone) by wooing.

- **_Win(verb)_** To achieve victory. _For example_: Who would win in a fight between an octopus and a dolphin?

- **_Win(verb)_** To obtain something that is wanted. _For example_: The company hopes to win an order from the government worth over 5 million dollars.

- **_Win(verb)_** To cause a victory for someone.

- **_win(noun)_** a victory (as in a race or other competition) "he was happy to get the win"

- ***win, winnings, profits(verb)*** something won (especially money)

- ***win(verb)*** be the winner in a contest or competition; be victorious "He won the Gold Medal in skating"; "Our home team won"; "Win the game"

- ***win, acquire, gain(verb)*** win something through one's efforts "I acquired a passing knowledge of Chinese"; "Gain an understanding of international finance"

- ***win, gain, advance, pull ahead, make headway, get ahead, gain ground(verb)*** obtain advantages, such as points, etc. "The home team was gaining ground"; "After defeating the Knicks, the Blazers pulled ahead of the Lakers in the battle for the number-one playoff berth in the Western Conference"

According to the British National Corpus

Spoken Corpus Frequency Rank popularity for the word 'WIN' in Spoken Corpus Frequency: #1285

Written Corpus Frequency Rank popularity for the word 'WIN' in Written Corpus Frequency: #1086

Nouns Frequency Rank popularity for the word 'WIN' in Nouns Frequency: #1419

Verbs Frequency Rank popularity for the word 'WIN' in Verbs Frequency: #90

- ***win, succeed, come through, bring home the bacon, deliver the goods(verb)*** attain success or reach a desired goal "The enterprise succeeded"; "We succeeded in getting tickets to the show"; "she struggled to overcome her handicap and won"

2. *Win–loss record*

In baseball and softball, a pitcher's win–loss record indicates the number of wins and losses they have been credited with. For example, a 20–10 win–loss record would represent 20 wins and 10 losses. In each game, one pitcher on the winning team is awarded a win and one pitcher on the losing team is given a loss in their respective statistics. These pitchers are collectively known as the pitchers of record. The designation of win or loss for a pitcher is known as a decision, and only one pitcher for each team receives a decision. A starting pitcher who does not receive credit for a win or loss is said to have no decision. In certain situations, another pitcher on the winning team who pitched in relief of the winning pitcher can be credited with a save, and holds can be awarded to relief pitchers on both sides, but these are never awarded to the same pitcher who is awarded the win. The official scorer of the game in accordance with the league's rules awards the decisions. The official scorer does not assign a winning or losing pitcher in some games, which are forfeited, such as those that are tied at the time of forfeiture.

3. What is a WIN

WIN is a three letters word that can mean any of the following:

WIN is Welfare Information Network

WIN is Windows

WIN is Winter

WIN is Microsoft Windows

WIN is Water Insoluble Nitrogen

WIN is Wine Is Not

WIN is Women in Nuclear

WIN is Wireless Information Network

WIN is Work It Now

WIN is What Is Normal

WIN is When In Need

WIN is Women In Need

WIN is Winn Dixie Stores, Inc.

WIN is Warfighter Information Network

WIN is Wireless Intelligent Network

WIN is Whip Inflation Now

WIN is What's Important Now

WIN is World Information Network

WIN is Women's Information Network

WIN is Western Integrated Networks

WIN is Workforce Investment Network

WIN is Wildlife Information Network

WIN is Women's International Net

WIN is Writing In Narrative

WIN is Whats Its Name

WIN is World Insurance Network

WIN is Www Irc Nl

WIN is Winton, Queensland, Australia

WIN is Waste Information Needs

WIN is Writing Improvement Network

WIN is Women's Individual Nutrition

WIN is
Westlaw Is
Natural

WIN is Window file (FoxPro - dBASE)

WIN is World Intercession Network

WIN is Western Information Network

WIN is Work In Newry

WIN is Women In Net

WIN is Way Into Nirvana

WIN is Women In Numbers

WIN is Whats Important Now

WIN is Western Integrated Network

WIN is Women Involved Now

WIN is Wireless Intelligence Network

WIN is Waardensegm enten In Nederland

WIN is White Indian Negro

WIN is Work Incentive Credit

WIN is Work Identification Number

WIN is Womens Information Network

WIN is Wisconsin Interstate Network

WIN is Word In Narrative

WIN is Women Inmate Nurturing

WIN is What Interpreters Need

WIN is West Islip Network

WIN is Wyoming Independent Newsletter

WIN is Womens International Net

WIN is Winnebago Indian News

WIN is Winning Individual Neighborhoods

WIN is Walking Is Nifty

WIN is WWMCCS Inter-computer Network

WIN is Wales Ireland And Norway

WIN is Words Images And Numbers

WIN is
Windows Icons
Nuts

WIN is Wake Information Network

WIN is Workers Independent News

WIN is Working Incident Number

WIN is Womans International Net

WIN is Wildcats In Nature

WIN is Western Industrial Nevada

WIN is Whatever Is Necessary

WIN is Wisconsin Involvement Network

WIN is What I Need

WIN is Wollongong Integrated Networks

WIN is Write In Nellie

WIN is Wash Identify Notify

WIN is Western Intertie Network

WIN is Worldwide Image Navigation

WIN is Workforce Innovation Networks

WIN is Wincanton (London Stock Exchange)

WIN is Work Incentive Network (Companies & Firms)

WIN is Working Image Network (Companies & Firms)

WIN is Women
In Networking

WIN is Women Investing Now

WIN is Wi-LAN Inc. (Private Company Symbol)

WIN is Welfare Information Network

4. Define Your WIN

NOW, Define your own and write it here. The most important is to follow your WIN.

- WIN is _____

- WIN is _____

- WIN is _____

5. ABOUT THE AUTHOR

Dr. Badawy is currently at the helm of IntelliView in the role of President and is navigating the company through commercialization into both local and international markets. He is also a world-leading researcher in video surveillance technology and continues to lecture throughout the world on his innovations. As a leading researcher he also oversees the evolution of the video surveillance technology developed at the University of Calgary and its commercialization in Calgary in order to serve and support Calgary businesses.

Dr. Badawy previously conducted his research at the U of Calgary, Canada where he was an iCore Chair Associate. Dr. Badawy developed a new model to describe optical video, thermal, infra-red, and 3D data in general. There he developed a model, algorithm, architecture and several platform implementations. These models have been granted several awards and patents, in addition to being published in numerous conference and journal papers. Dr. Badawy also trained and mentored researchers and engineers on his new technology, leading them to a successful commercialization path through a University Spin-off which housed 12 co-founders who worked in his research team at the U of C. Dr. Badawy's innovation and leadership contributed to Canada with:

• More than 400 technical papers that have been accepted for publication by the internal peer community, and a large number of citations that use this work, which currently exceeds 3000 citations.

• The 50+ contributions to developing the ISO standards, which represent more than 75% of the hardware reference model for the H.264 compression standard. Dr. Badawy led the development of the hardware reference model for MPEG-4, Part 9 in collaboration with Xilinx and EPFL. Also, he worked to develop several motion tracking architectures for low power applications that can be integrated into system-on-a-chip applications. This contribution impacted all international companies developing video products, as they have to use the developed reference model for standards conformance tests.

• Dr. Badawy was also listed as a "Primary contributor" in the VSI Alliance™ for developing the "Platform-Based Design Definitions and Taxonomy, (PBD 11.0), 2003". VSI Alliance is an industrial organization aimed at the development of a standard for IP Cores. This standard is used as a reference by all companies developing electronic chips for different applications, though mainly for communications and video.

- The impact of his publications has an h-index of 10 according to SCOPUS.COM, with the largest number of citations being 59, with total citations being 278, and about 1000 citations in Google. His success is product of his willingness to accept responsibility.
- The commercialization of a Canadian Video technology through a spin-off company IntelliView Technologies Inc.

All of this training, knowledge and technology that Dr. Badawy has transferred over the last ten years is seen in his students (about 2,000 undergraduate and 50 graduate), who are now contributing to the engineering field in different capacities, ranging from design, teaching, supervising, and manufacturing in several electronic components.